Inquiry Journal

Level 2

A Division of The McGraw-Hill Companies

Columbus, Ohio

www.sra4kids.com

SRA/McGraw-Hill

*A Division of The **McGraw·Hill** Companies*

Copyright © 2002 by SRA/McGraw-Hill.

Send all inquiries to:
SRA/McGraw-Hill
8787 Orion Place
Columbus, OH 43240-4027

Printed in the United States of America.

ISBN 0-07-569565-0

8 9 QPD 07 06 05

Table of Contents

Knowledge About Sharing Stories

- This is what I know about sharing stories before reading the unit.

  _____

  _____

  _____

  _____

- These are some things I would like to know about sharing stories.

  _____

  _____

  _____

  _____

  Reminder: I should read this page again when I get to the end of the unit to see how much I've learned about sharing stories.

UNIT 1 Sharing Stories

Recording Concept Information

As I read each story, this is what I found out about sharing stories.

- "Ant and the Three Little Figs" by Betsy Byars

_____

_____

_____

_____

_____

- "Come Back, Jack!"
  by Catherine and Laurence Anholt

_____

_____

_____

_____

_____

- "The Library" by Sarah Stewart

_____

_____

_____

_____

_____

_____

- "Story Hour—Starring Megan!"
  by Julie Brillhart

_____

_____

_____

_____

_____

_____

- "Tomás and the Library Lady" by Pat Mora

_____

_____

_____

_____

_____

_____

_____

My Favorite Stories

Use the lines below to write about your three favorite stories.

Title: _____

Author: _____

Why I liked this story: _____

_____

_____

Title: _____

Author: _____

Why I liked this story: _____

_____

_____

Title: _____

Author: _____

Why I liked this story: _____

_____

_____

UNIT 1 Sharing Stories

Alphabetical Order

Rules for Alphabetical order:

1. When words start with different letters, use the first letter of each word to put the words in alphabetical order.
2. When words start with the same first letter, use the next letter that is different in each word to put the words in alphabetical order.

- Put these words from the story "Ant and the Three Little Figs" in alphabetical order.

me   I   you   the   he   it

_____

_____

- Put these words from the story in alphabetical order. Which letter of each word will you use?

said   say   story

_____

_____

_____

- Put these words from the story in alphabetical order.

Ant   all   pig   once   fig   oh

_____

_____

_____

_____

_____

- Write five words of your own. Then write them again in alphabetical order.

_____   _____

_____   _____

_____   _____

_____   _____

UNIT 1 Sharing Stories

Comparing Stories

Stories are often retold by different writers. Read the same story by two different writers. Record how they are alike and how they are different.

Comparing Stories	
Story Titles: _____ _____	
How they are alike	**How they are different**

Recording Questions

What would you like to know about sharing stories? Write your questions or ideas here.

_____

_____

_____

_____

_____

Where can you look for ideas about sharing stories?

_____

_____

_____

_____

UNIT 1 Sharing Stories

Planning Your Investigation

How can you investigate sharing stories? You may have already started asking questions to find out what stories mean to people and what kinds of stories they like. What else can you ask?

_____

_____

_____

_____

As you begin your investigation of sharing stories, you will want to keep a list of things you need to do. Check off each item as you finish it. Here is a start of a list of things you might want to do. Add to it as you read the unit.

Things to Do

☐ Talk to friends about stories they like

☐ Talk to adults about stories

☐ Find books of stories

☐ _____

☐ _____

☐ _____

Parts of a Book

You can find all kinds of important information in books when you know where to look. Pick one of your textbooks and use what you have learned about the parts of a book to find the following information.

- Title of book: _____

- Author: _____

- Copyright date: _____

- Does the table of contents show chapters,

  units, or story titles? _____

  How many are there? _____

  Write the name of one and the page on which it begins.

  _____

  _____

- Does your book have a glossary? _____

  If yes, what is the first word listed? _____

- Does your book have an index? _____

  If yes, on what page does it begin? _____

UNIT 1 Sharing Stories

Interview

What questions will you ask in your interview with the librarian? On these pages, write the questions you will ask. As you ask each question during the interview, use the space below the question to write the answer.

1. Question: _____

_____

    Answer: _____

_____

2. Question: _____

_____

    Answer: _____

_____

3. Question: _____

_____

    Answer: _____

_____

4. Question: _____

_____

Answer: _____

_____

5. Question: _____

_____

Answer: _____

_____

6. Question: _____

_____

Answer: _____

_____

7. Question: _____

_____

Answer: _____

_____

Asking Questions

Read and answer each question. Then write the question in a different way so that it cannot be answered by the words *yes* or *no*. Then answer your new question.

1. Do you like books? _____

   New Question: _____

   _____

   _____

2. Do you have books? _____

   New Question: _____

   _____

   _____

3. Do you read? _____

   _____

   New Question: _____

   _____

   _____

Look again at the questions you wrote on pages 12–13 of the *Inquiry Journal.* Which questions can you make better? On the lines below, write each question you think you can make better. Then rewrite each question.

_____

_____

_____

_____

_____

_____

_____

_____

_____

_____

_____

Parts to the Library or Media Center

Look at the list below. Where can you find each of these in your library or media center? Draw a map of your library on the next page by drawing a box where each of these items can be found in your library. Label each box so you know what it stands for. If your library doesn't have one of the items, leave it out of your map.

Parts of our library:
- The front door, or entrance
- Librarian's desk
- Card catalog (or computer catalog)
- Computers
- Places to sit and read
- Picture books
- Story books (fiction)
- Biographies
- Nonfiction
- Technology books
- Books for older students
- Records, CDs, tapes
- Movies
- Computer programs

If there are places or things in your library that are not on the list, add them to the list and to your map.

Using the Card Catalog

1. Find and mark these items on the catalog card shown:
   - Circle the call number.
   - Draw a line under the author's name.
   - Draw two lines under the subject.
   - Put a check mark by the title.

E
599.74422BEN

Bender, Lionel
Lions and Tigers
New York, Gloucester Press, c. 1988
   [31]p.

Summary: Describes the habits and
   behavior of lions and tigers, with a
   discussion of how they survive.

1. lions   2. tigers

---

2. Use the card or computer catalog to find one
   book on a subject you are interested in. Copy
   the call number, the author's name, and the
   book title onto a piece of paper. Then take
   the paper with you as you look for the book.

Unit Wrap-Up

- How did you feel about this unit?

  ☐ I enjoyed it very much. ☐ I liked it.

  ☐ I liked some of it. ☐ I didn't like it.

- Was the unit easy or hard?

  ☐ easy ☐ medium ☐ hard

- Did you learn much during the unit?

  ☐ I learned a lot about sharing stories.

  ☐ I learned a few new things about sharing stories.

  ☐ I didn't learn very much at all.

- Explain your last answer.

  _____

  _____

  _____

- What was the most interesting thing that you learned about sharing stories?

  _____

  _____

- What did you learn about sharing stories that you didn't know before?

_____

_____

_____

- What did you learn about yourself as a learner?

_____

_____

_____

- What did you have to work on to become a better learner?

_____

_____

_____

- Which resources, such as books, magazines, interviews, and the Internet, did you use on your own as you investigated sharing stories? Which was the most useful? Why?

_____

_____

_____

Name _____ Date _____

Knowledge About Kindness

- This is what I know about kindness before reading the unit.

_____

_____

_____

_____

- These are some things I would like to know about kindness.

_____

_____

_____

_____

Reminder: I should read this page again when I get to the end of the unit to see how much I've learned about kindness.

UNIT 2 Kindness

Recording Concept Information

As I read each story, this is what I found out about kindness.

- "Mushroom in the Rain" by Mirra Ginsburg

_____

_____

_____

_____

_____

- "The Elves and the Shoemaker"
  retold by Freya Littledale

_____

_____

_____

_____

_____

- "The Paper Crane" by Molly Bang

_____

_____

_____

_____

- "Butterfly House" by Eve Bunting

_____

_____

_____

_____

- "Corduroy" by Don Freeman

_____

_____

_____

_____

- "The Story of Three Whales" by Giles Whittell

_____

_____

_____

_____

_____

_____

- "Cinderella" retold by Fabio Coen

_____

_____

_____

_____

_____

_____

_____

Name _____ Date _____

Courtesy, Rule, Law

Use the box below to record examples of
courtesies, rules, and laws.

Courtesy	Rule (home or classroom)	Law
Treat other people's things with respect	Ask before borrowing from a classmate	Stealing is against the law

Recording Questions

What would you like to know about kindness?
Write your questions or ideas here.

_____

_____

_____

_____

_____

_____

Where can you look for ideas about kindness?

_____

_____

_____

_____

Planning Your Investigation

How can you investigate kindness? You may have already started asking questions, such as what are examples of kindness. What else can you ask?

_____

_____

_____

As you begin exploring kindness, keep a list of things you need to do. Check off each item as you finish it. Here is a start. Add to it as you read the unit.

☐ Talk to friends about what being kind means

☐ Talk to adults about kindness

☐ Find and read books or stories about people or characters who show kindness

☐ _____

☐ _____

☐ _____

UNIT 2 Kindness

Summarizing and Organizing Information

- Write a topic related to kindness that you

  want to find out more about. _____

- List some things you already know about
  your topic.

  _____

  _____

  _____

- What do you want to find out about your topic?

  Who: _____

  What: _____

  _____

  When: _____

  Where: _____

  _____

  How: _____

  _____

- Find books or magazines about your topic.
  Read them and write what you learn here.
  Use your own words.

Who: _____

_____

What: _____

_____

_____

When: _____

_____

Where: _____

_____

How: _____

_____

_____

Other information: _____

_____

_____

_____

Recording Acts of Kindness

Pay close attention to how people act toward each other each day. Record acts of kindness that you see.

Kind Act	Where did it happen?	Why did it happen?	How did the person react?	How did it make you feel?

- On a separate sheet of paper, tell how you feel about the kind acts you have seen.

Making Observations

Write your teacher's questions and your answers on the lines.

1. Question: _____

   _____

   Answer: _____

   _____

2. Question: _____

   _____

   Answer: _____

   _____

3. Question: _____

   _____

   Answer: _____

   _____

4. Question: _____

   _____

   Answer: _____

Choose one act of kindness that you saw someone do. Write about it below.

The act of kindness I saw was: _____

_____

_____

_____

Questions I have about what I saw: _____

_____

_____

_____

These are the details I noticed: _____

_____

_____

_____

_____

_____

_____

Groups That Help People

Find out about groups that help people in need. Record the information you gather.

Who did you talk to? _____

_____

What group does this person work for? _____

_____

How does the group help people? _____

_____

Where does the group get the things they give to

people in need? _____

_____

_____

How do people get the things this group offers?

_____

_____

UNIT 2 Kindness

Where Does the Food Go?

Person interviewed	Name of business	What happens to leftover food

Work with your classmates to think of ways leftover food might be used rather than thrown out. Write your suggestions here.

_____

_____

_____

Following Directions

In "The Paper Crane," the stranger makes a crane from a paper napkin. Origami is the art of folding paper. People who do origami must follow directions to make sure that the sculpture comes out correctly.

- Think of something you know how to do well. It may be a chore, a craft, or a game. Write the name of the task you do well here.

_____

- What are the steps for your task? Write the steps below.

_____

_____

_____

_____

_____

- Look over the steps. Are they in the correct order? Put numbers next to each step to show which is first, next, and so on.

Following Directions *(continued)*

- Now write each step clearly in the correct order. Use complete sentences. Draw a picture to go with each step.

1._____

_____

2._____

_____

3._____

_____

4._____

_____

Helping Wildlife

Fill in the chart with information you find about helping wildlife.

Animal	Problem	Helpful	Harmful

Charts and Diagrams

In "Butterfly House," you read about a little house built for a butterfly. Look at the chart and diagram below. They tell about how you could build a butterfly house.

Butterfly House

Use the diagram and chart to complete the sentences or to answer the questions about how to build a butterfly house.

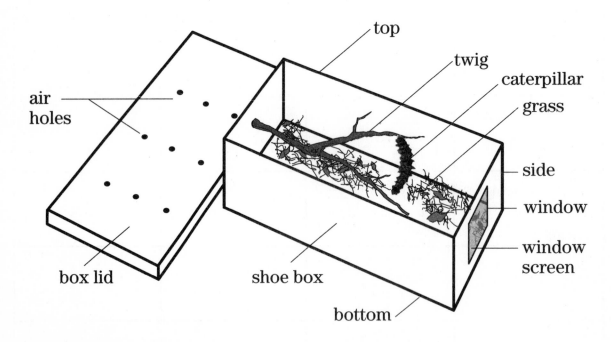

Length	13 inches
Width	5 inches
Height	4 inches
Decorations	

1. Air holes should be placed in the _____ .

2. What should be put in the bottom of the butterfly house?

   _____

3. How long should the butterfly house be?

   _____

4. The window should be placed _____
   of the house.

5. How high should the box be? _____

6. A _____ should be placed in
   the box with the grass.

7. A _____ should be placed
   over the window.

   Decide how you would decorate your
butterfly house. Then write what you would
do in the space in the chart.

Brainstorm a Toy Drive

What do you think will need to be done to have a successful toy drive? Work with your classmates to fill in the web organizer below. Write the tasks you think will have to be done.

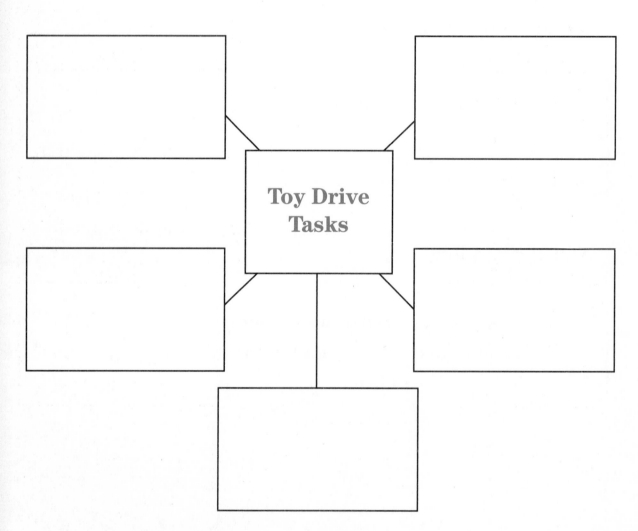

Toy Drive Tasks

Add any additional tasks you think of after talking with your classmates.

_____

_____

Organize Information

What do you think will need to be done to complete your kindness investigation? Work with your group to fill in the web organizer below. Write the name of your project in the middle box. Then write the tasks that you need to do in the other boxes.

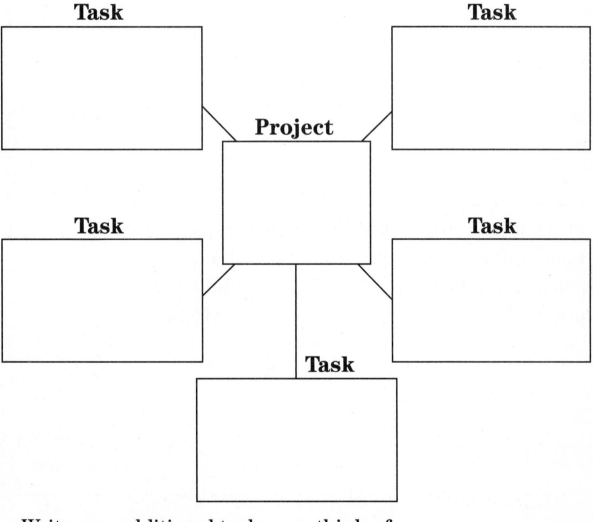

Write any additional tasks you think of.

_____

_____

Organize the tasks you need to do in the order that they need to be done.

1. _____

2. _____

3. _____

4. _____

5. _____

6. _____

7. _____

8. _____

Check your list. Is there anything you forgot? If you follow the steps on your list, will your investigation be complete? Write anything you forgot. Then decide when it would need to be done.

_____

_____

_____

_____

_____

Using Newspapers and Magazines

Find a story or article in a newspaper or magazine. Then answer the questions below.

Is your article from a newspaper or a magazine? _____

_____

Name and date of newspaper or magazine: _____

_____

Name of article and page it starts on: _____

_____

How many pages is the article? _____

How could you tell what page to go to next? _____

_____

What is the article about? _____

_____

_____

UNIT 2 Kindness

Solving a Problem

State a problem with meanness or jealousy you have had. Then write possible solutions to the problem.

Write the problem. _____

_____

_____

How did you react? _____

_____

_____

What else could you have done? _____

_____

_____

Ask a friend what he or she would have done. _____

_____

_____

If this happened again, what would you do? _____

_____

_____

Using a Dictionary and Glossary

Dictionaries are books that include thousands of words and their meanings.

A **glossary** is a part of a book, usually at the end, that contains only words that are in that book.

About Dictionaries and Glossaries

1. The words are listed in alphabetical order.

2. The words are spelled correctly.

3. Each word is defined or given a meaning.

4. Guide words tell the first and last words on a page.

Look up the following words from "Cinderella" in the glossary of your anthology and in a dictionary. Write the guide words from each source.

1. **cellar**

   glossary   _____   _____

   dictionary _____   _____

2. **wand**

   glossary   _____   _____

   dictionary _____   _____

3. **gown**

glossary _____   _____

dictionary _____   _____

Sometimes it is important to find a word quickly in the dictionary. In your mind, divide the dictionary into three parts: a beginning, a middle, and an end. Words are found in different parts, depending on their first letter.

Locator Chart	
A–F words	Beginning of the dictionary
G–Q words	Middle of the dictionary
R–Z words	End of the dictionary

In the space next to each word, write which part of the dictionary the word can be found. Use the Locator Chart to help you. The first one is done for you.

1. **hero** _____middle_____   7. **whistle** _____

2. **brave** _____   8. **jumbo** _____

3. **courage** _____   9. **tiny** _____

4. **guts** _____   10. **enormous** _____

5. **swatted** _____   11. **pinkies** _____

6. **pavement** _____   12. **large** _____

Unit Wrap-Up

- How did you like this unit?

  ☐ I really enjoyed it.   ☐ I liked it.

  ☐ I liked some of it.   ☐ I didn't like it.

- Was the unit easy or hard?

  ☐ easy   ☐ medium   ☐ hard

- Did you learn much during the unit?

  ☐ I learned a lot about kindness.

  ☐ I learned a few new things about kindness.

  ☐ I didn't learn very much at all.

- Explain your last answer.

  _____

  _____

  _____

- What was the most interesting thing that you learned about kindness?

  _____

  _____

  _____

- What did you learn about kindness that you didn't know before?

_____

_____

_____

- What did you learn about yourself as a learner?

_____

_____

_____

- What did you have to work on to become a better learner?

_____

_____

_____

- Which resources, such as books, magazines, interviews, and the Internet, did you use on your own as you investigated kindness? Which was the most useful? Why?

_____

_____

Knowledge About Animal Camouflage

- This is what I know about animal camouflage
  before reading the unit.

_____

_____

_____

_____

_____

- These are some things I would like to know
  about animal camouflage.

_____

_____

_____

_____

_____

Reminder: I should read this page again when
I get to the end of the unit to see how much I've
learned about animal camouflage.

Recording Concept Information

As I read each story, this is what I found out about animal camouflage.

• "I See Animals Hiding" by Jim Arnosky

_____

_____

_____

_____

_____

• "They Thought They Saw Him"
by Craig Kee Strete

_____

_____

_____

_____

_____

- "Hungry Little Hare" by Howard Goldsmith

_____

_____

_____

_____

_____

_____

- "How to Hide an Octopus and Other Sea Creatures" by Ruth Heller

_____

_____

_____

_____

_____

_____

- "How the Guinea Fowl Got Her Spots"
  retold by Barbara Knutson

_____

_____

_____

_____

_____

- "Animal Camouflage" by Janet McDonnell

_____

_____

_____

_____

_____

Possible Questions to Investigate

- Write your possible questions on the lines.

_____

_____

_____

_____

_____

_____

_____

_____

_____

_____

_____

_____

_____

_____

_____

_____

UNIT 3 Look Again

Choosing an Investigation Question

A good question for our group to investigate: _____

_____

_____

_____

Why this is an interesting investigation question: _____

_____

_____

_____

Some other questions: _____

_____

_____

_____

As you talk about the investigation question with your group, the question will change. Return to this page to record any new questions and changes.

Charts

Look through "I See Animals Hiding" and fill in the chart with information about the animals and how they use camouflage.

Animal Camouflage		
Animal	Changes color?	How it hides

Think about the questions you want to investigate. Write the title of a chart you could make to help you with your unit investigation.

_____

_____

Animals That Use Camouflage

In "They Thought They Saw Him," a chameleon fooled many animals by blending in with the background. These American chameleons can be found in the southeastern part of the United States. Choose five animals from "I See Animals Hiding" and find out where in the United States the animals live. Then fill in the chart. The first one is done for you. Then answer *yes* or *no* to tell whether or not the animal lives in your state.

Animal	Where the animal lives	Does this animal live in your state?
chameleon	SE United States (American chameleon)	

Investigation Planning

Use the calendar to help plan your camouflage unit investigation. Fill in the dates. Make sure that you mark any days you know you will not be able to work on the

Sunday	Monday	Tuesday	Wednesday

Investigation Planning *(continued)*

investigation. Then choose the date on which you will start and the date on which you hope to finish. You may also find it helpful to mark the dates by which you hope to complete different parts of the investigation. Record what you accomplish each day.

Thursday	Friday	Saturday

Our Idea (or Conjecture)

Part 1

Investigation question: _____

_____

_____

_____

First idea, or conjecture: _____

_____

_____

_____

Part 2

Revised investigation question: _____

_____

_____

Revised idea, or conjecture: _____

_____

_____

_____

Globes and Atlases

A globe is a three-dimensional model of Earth.
Look at the illustration of a globe below. Then
follow the directions.

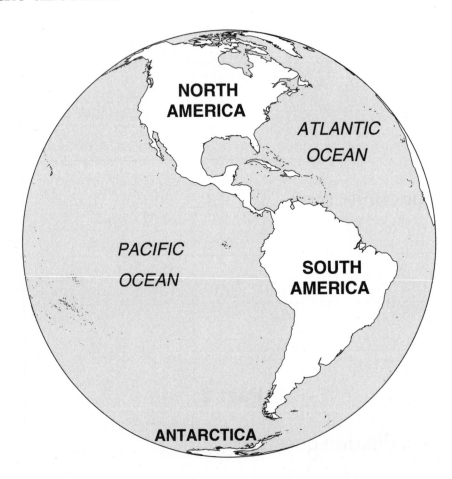

1. List the oceans that you can see on the globe.

_____

2. Color all the water blue.

3. Color North America red.

4. Color South America brown.

5. Color Antarctica yellow.

An atlas is a book of maps. These can include maps of small areas, like a state, or large areas like the world. By looking at the picture below, you will notice that these atlas pages look like a flattened globe.

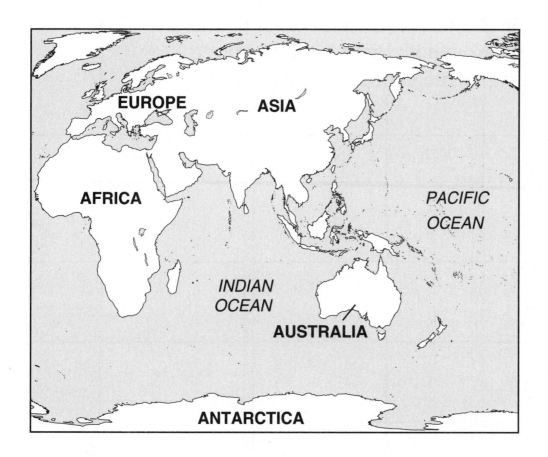

1. Color all the water blue.
2. Color Australia green.
3. Color Africa brown.
4. Color Europe purple.
5. Color Asia orange.
6. Color Antarctica yellow.

Making Observations

Record the animals you find on your field trip. Describe the place you found the animal. Then tell what the animal looked like. Did it blend into the area around it? Did it look like a tree limb or a twig? Write your findings in the chart.

Animal	Where I found it	What it looked like

Pick one of the animals you found. Then tell why it was hard or easy to find.

_____

_____

_____

Needs and Plans

My group's investigation question:

_____

_____

Knowledge Needs—Information I need to find or figure out to help investigate the question:

A. _____

_____

B. _____

_____

C. _____

_____

D. _____

_____

E. _____

_____

Source	Useful?	How?
Encyclopedias		
Books		
Magazines		
Newspapers		
Videotapes, filmstrips, etc.		
Television		
Interviews, observations		
Museums		
Other		

Group Plan

Our investigation question and conjecture:

_____

_____

_____

Group Members	Main Jobs

Name_____ Date_____

Taking Notes

As your classmate tells about his or her topic, take notes on what is said. Remember,
- Write only the most important things.
- Make each new idea a new line.
- Write in words or phrases instead of whole sentences.
- Write neatly so that you can read your notes.
- Write questions that you think of as you take notes.

What the talk is about: _____

_____

Important idea: _____

_____

Important idea: _____

_____

Important idea: _____

_____

Questions I have about the talk: _____

_____

_____

Using Maps

Here are some important features that help you use maps to find information.

- The **title** is the name of the map and tells what it is about.
- The **key** tells what the special symbols or colors on the map mean.
- The **scale** gives you the information you need to measure the map and tell the distance in miles between two points.
- The **direction arrows,** or **compass rose,** show north, south, east, and west on the map.

Look in a social studies book or an atlas to find a map.

What kind of information does your map tell? _____

_____

Draw two pictures that were shown in the map key. Tell what they mean.

Pictures   **Meanings**

_____

_____

Name one place on the map. _____

_____

Name another place on the map. _____

_____

Look at the compass rose. Then tell whether the second place is north, south, east, or west of the first place.

_____

Use the map scale to tell how many miles away the second place is from the first place.

_____

Types of Camouflage

Look back over the selections you have read. Name some animals and tell how they camouflage themselves.

Animal	Camouflage

Which animals use the same kind of camouflage?

_____

_____

Which animals use a different way to camouflage themselves?

_____

_____

Camouflage Yourself

Pick three places where you go often. Write what you would have to do to camouflage yourself in each place.

Place	Camouflage

Which would be the easiest place to camouflage yourself? Explain why.

_____

_____

Which would be the hardest place to camouflage yourself? Explain why.

_____

_____

Skimming

Choose a magazine article or a chapter from your social studies book. Skim the selection and answer the questions.

1. What is the title of the article or chapter? _____

_____

2. Are there any headings?_____

3. Write two headings you find in the selection. _____

_____

4. What do the headings help you to know? _____

_____

_____

5. Are there any pictures with captions? _____

6. What do the pictures and captions help you to know?

_____

_____

7. What special features does the article have? _____

_____

_____

Unit Wrap-Up

- How did you like this unit?

  ☐ I really enjoyed it. ☐ I liked it.

  ☐ I liked some of it. ☐ I didn't like it.

- Was the unit easy or hard?

  ☐ easy   ☐ medium   ☐ hard

- Did you learn much during the unit?

  ☐ I learned a lot about animal camouflage.

  ☐ I learned a few new things about animal camouflage.

  ☐ I didn't learn very much at all.

- Explain your last answer.

  _____

  _____

  _____

- What was the most interesting thing that you learned about animal camouflage?

  _____

  _____

  _____

- What did you learn about animal camouflage that you didn't know before?

_____

_____

_____

- What did you learn about yourself as a learner?

_____

_____

_____

- What did you have to work on to become a better learner?

_____

_____

_____

- Which resources, such as books, magazines, interviews, and the Internet, did you use on your own as you investigated animal camouflage? Which was the most useful? Why?

_____

_____

_____

UNIT 4 Fossils

Knowledge About Fossils

- This is what I know about fossils before reading the unit.

_____

_____

_____

_____

_____

- Here are some things I would like to know about fossils.

_____

_____

_____

_____

Reminder: I should read this page again after we finish the unit to discover how much I learned about fossils.

Recording Concept Information

As I read each story, here is what I found out about fossils.

- "Fossils Tell of Long Ago" by Aliki

_____

_____

_____

_____

_____

- "The Dinosaur Who Lived in My Backyard" by B. G. Hennessy

_____

_____

_____

_____

_____

- "Dinosaur Fossils" by Dr. Alvin Granowsky

_____

_____

_____

_____

_____

_____

- "Why Did the Dinosaurs Disappear?"
  by Karen Sapp

_____

_____

_____

_____

_____

_____

_____

- "Monster Tracks" by Barbara Bruno

_____

_____

_____

_____

_____

- "Let's Go Dinosaur Tracking!"
  by Miriam Schlein

_____

_____

_____

_____

_____

What Do Fossils Tell?

Fossils can give clues to what life was like long, long ago. If you found a fossil, what questions would you ask about it? What might you learn from the fossil about the past?

These are some questions I would have about the fossil:

_____

_____

_____

_____

This is what my fossil might tell me about the past:

_____

_____

_____

_____

Choosing an Investigation Question

A good question for our group to investigate: _____

_____

_____

_____

Why this is an interesting investigation question: _____

_____

_____

_____

Some new questions: _____

_____

_____

_____

   As you talk about the investigation question
with your group, the question will change.
Return to this page to record any new questions.

Using an Encyclopedia

Use this page to find and record information from an encyclopedia about your investigation.

Guidelines for Using an Encyclopedia

1. Find the index of an encyclopedia. Find your subject in the index.
2. Write down the name of the encyclopedia, the subject name, the volume numbers or letters, and page numbers listed for the subject.
3. Find the articles in the encyclopedia and skim them.
4. Look at the end of each article for other places to find more information about your subject.

Fill in the following information for a question you are investigating.

My question: _____

Name of encyclopedia, subject, volume numbers (or letters),

and page numbers: _____

_____

_____

Other articles or books about my subject: _____

_____

Living in the Days of Dinosaurs

From reading "The Dinosaur Who Lived in My Backyard," you have learned that a dinosaur would have a really hard time fitting into the human world. How would you have fit into the dinosaur's world? The questions below can help you think about it.

- How I think the world looked during the time of the dinosaurs:

_____

_____

_____

- What I would have liked about living in the time of the dinosaurs:

_____

_____

- What problems I would have had if I had lived in the time of the dinosaurs:

_____

_____

Investigation Planning

Use the calendar to help plan your fossils unit investigation. Fill in the dates. Make sure that you mark any days you know you will not be able to work on the investigation. Then choose the date on which you will start and the date on

Sunday	Monday	Tuesday	Wednesday

which you hope to finish. You may also find it helpful to mark the dates by which you hope to complete different parts of the investigation. Record what you accomplish each day.

Thursday	Friday	Saturday

UNIT 4 Fossils

Our Idea (or Conjecture)

Part 1

Investigation question: _____

_____

_____

_____

First idea, or conjecture: _____

_____

_____

_____

Part 2

Revised investigation question: _____

_____

_____

Revised idea, or conjecture: _____

_____

_____

Using the Card Catalog

In the card catalog, find the titles of three books on a subject that you are investigating. Write the title, the author's name, and the location code for each book. Then on your own, or with the help of someone at the library, find these books.

Title: _____

Author's name: _____

Code: _____

Title: _____

Author's name: _____

Code: _____

Title: _____

Author's name: _____

Code: _____

Fossil Web

Add information you have found about fossils to the web.

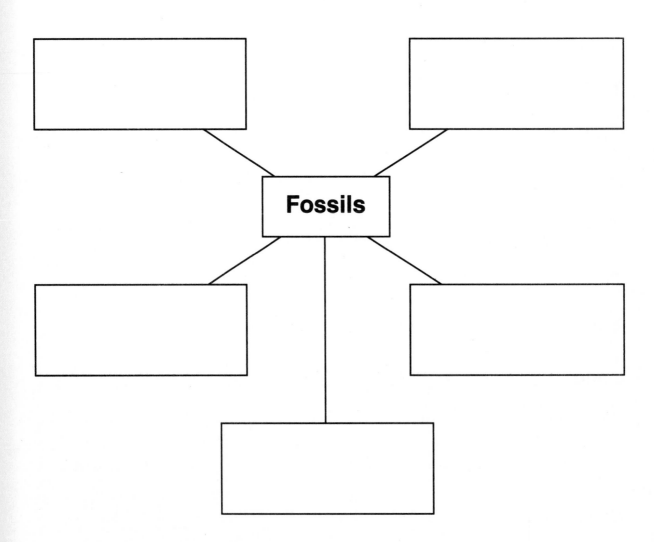

Needs and Plans

My group's question:

_____

_____

Knowledge Needs—Information I need to find
or figure out to help investigate the question:

A. _____

_____

B. _____

_____

C. _____

_____

D. _____

_____

E. _____

_____

Source	Useful?	How?
Encyclopedias		
Books		
Magazines		
Newspapers		
Videotapes, filmstrips, etc.		
Television		
Interviews, observations		
Museums		
Other		

Group Plan

Our investigation question:

_____

_____

Who will do which job?

Group Members	Main Jobs

UNIT 4 Fossils

Table of Contents/Index

Use the table of contents and the index in books to help you find the information you are looking for. Do the following:

- First, find a book on your subject.
- Then look in the table of contents. Find a chapter that may have information that you need.
- Write the chapter title and the page number below. If you find more than one chapter with information that you need, write the title and page number of each one.
- Think of words that name the information you're looking for. Then look through the index of the book. Find words related to your subject. Write the page numbers.

Book title: _____

Titles of chapters and page numbers with information I need:

_____

_____ Page: _____

_____

_____ Page: _____

Words related to the information I'm looking for and
the page numbers from the index:

_____

_____ Page: _____

_____

_____ Page: _____

_____

_____ Page: _____

UNIT 4 Fossils

Ask an Expert

These pages will help you to write good
questions to ask the expert.

- Write the topic about fossils that interests you.

_____

_____

- Now think about your topic. What do you
  wonder about? Write any questions you can
  think of.

_____

_____

_____

_____

_____

_____

_____

- Reread each question you wrote. Cross out any question you think will not give you much information.

- Cross out any question you think will give you too much information.

- Cross out any question that is not about the topic you wrote at the beginning of this exercise.

- Write the questions that are left.

_____

_____

_____

_____

_____

_____

_____

_____

_____

Time Lines

- Each mark on a time line represents a date.

- Each mark represents a single event.

- Events are listed on the time line from left to right in the order in which they happened. The earliest event appears at the far left.

  Use "Why Did the Dinosaurs Disappear?" to number the events below in the correct order. Then on the line below, make a time line with the information.

_____ Meat-eaters could not find plant-eating dinosaurs to eat.

_____ New plants started growing.

_____ The new plants poisoned the plant-eating dinosaurs.

_____ The climate changed.

_____

Track Tales

Tracks can tell many things about an animal.
Write three things that you can learn by looking
at an animal's tracks.

1. _____

2. _____

3. _____

Write three things that a scientist can learn
about prehistoric animals by looking at track
fossils.

1. _____

_____

2. _____

_____

3. _____

_____

Recording Data

Use the chart below to record information or data about objects you use every day. Choose objects such as a piece of clothing, a book, a toy, or any other handy object and fill in as much information about the objects as you can.

Object	Color	Weight	Shape	Height	Length

Unit Wrap-Up

- How did you like this unit?

  ☐ I really enjoyed it.   ☐ I liked it.

  ☐ I liked some of it.   ☐ I didn't like it.

- Was the unit easy or hard?

  ☐ easy   ☐ medium   ☐ hard

- Did you learn much during the unit?

  ☐ I learned a lot about fossils.

  ☐ I learned a few new things about fossils.

  ☐ I didn't learn very much at all.

- Explain your last answer.

  _____

  _____

  _____

- What was the most interesting thing that you learned about fossils?

  _____

  _____

  _____

- What did you learn about fossils that you didn't know before?

  _____

  _____

  _____

- What did you learn about yourself as a learner?

  _____

  _____

  _____

- What did you have to work on to become a better learner?

  _____

  _____

  _____

- Which resources, such as books, magazines, interviews, and the Internet, did you use on your own as you investigated fossils? Which was the most useful? Why?

  _____

  _____

4. Question: _____

_____

_____

Answer: _____

_____

_____

_____

5. Question: _____

_____

_____

Answer: _____

_____

_____

6. Question: _____

_____

_____

Answer: _____

_____

_____

Qualities of a Brave Person

From your reading you have learned that maybe a quality of bravery is being able to be brave even though one doesn't feel brave. Find out what other qualities a brave person is expected to have. Look through books, magazines, and newspapers or ask people what qualities they expect to find in a brave person. List the qualities and tell why these qualities are important.

Qualities of a Brave Person   **Explain**

Qualities of a Brave Person   **Explain**

You may wish to pick one of the qualities that a brave person would have and draw a picture to show it. For example, if you think that honesty is a quality of a brave person, draw a picture that comes to mind when you think about a person who is being honest.

UNIT 5 Courage

Planning Your Investigation

How can you further investigate being brave? You may have already started asking questions to find out when people need to be brave, what they need to be brave about, and what people think "being brave" means. What else can you ask?

_____

_____

_____

_____

_____

As you begin your investigation of courage, you will want to keep a list of things you need to do. Check off each item as you finish it. Here is the start of a list of things you might want to do. Add to it as you read the unit.

Things to Do

☐ Talk to friends

☐ Talk to adults

☐ Find and use books from bibliographies

☐ _____

☐ _____

☐ _____

Reading a Map

The United States is a land of people, many of whose families came from different countries all over the world. It might have been our parents, or grandparents, or great-great-great grandparents who moved to the United States. It took a lot of courage for them to move. Have you ever moved? Has your family ever moved from one state to another? Would you like to travel one day to another country or state? Use the classroom maps your teacher provides to answer the questions below.

Use the map of the world to answer questions 1–5. Use the map of the Unites States to answer questions 6–10.

1. List three oceans that you see on the world map.

   _____   _____

   _____

2. Write five countries that you see on the world map.

   _____   _____

   _____   _____

   _____

3. If you know, write the name of the country your family came from. (You could ask your parents if you don't know.) What continent is that country on? Write the name.

_____

4. Describe the path your family might have traveled to move to the United States. For example, if they came from a country in Asia, they might have had to travel across a part of Asia, then across Europe, then across the Atlantic Ocean.

_____

_____

_____

_____

5. If you could travel some day to another country, what country would that be? Is that country north, south, east, or west (or a combination of two of these directions, such as northwest) of the United States?

_____

_____

6. Write the names of two lakes you see on the map of the United States.

_____

_____

7. What country is next to the United States in the north? What country is next to the United States in the south?

_____

_____

8. Write the name of the state where you live. What other states or sea or ocean lie next to your state?

_____

_____

_____

9. Look at the map's legend. Describe or draw a picture of one symbol in the legend. What does it stand for? Give an example of this symbol being used on the map.

_____

_____

_____

10. If your family has ever moved from one state to another, write the name of the state where you moved from. Write the name of the state where you moved to. Is the state where you moved to north, south, east, or west (or a combination of two of these directions, such as southeast) of the state where you used to live?

_____

_____

_____

_____

How to Take Notes

1. Use a different page for each different kind of information.

2. Make a heading for each kind of information. You may have many facts under one heading.

3. Sum up an author's ideas in your own words. Write down key phrases or short sentences. Do not just copy down the author's words.

4. Once in a while you may use an author's exact words in your notes. Always put the author's words within quotation marks. Then, write down the author's name, the book title (or magazine and article titles), and the page number of the quotation.

5. Write down only the most important facts and ideas.

6. Write neatly.

   Find information on your investigation question. Write down the most important ideas and facts.

Investigation question: _____

_____

First heading: _____

Notes: _____

_____

_____

_____

Second heading: _____

Notes: _____

_____

_____

_____

Third heading: _____

Notes: _____

_____

_____

_____

Bar Graphs

A *bar graph* uses lines or bars to show information. You can use a bar graph to show how many people have a certain opinion or have done a certain thing. You can also compare information on a bar graph.

- Decide what question you are going to ask people. Remember to ask a question that can have a short answer like "yes," "no," or "I don't know."

_____

_____

_____

- Record your answers or results. How many people answered the question each way it could be answered?

_____

_____

_____

- Give your graph a title.

- Write the possible answers along the left side of the bar graph.

Bar Graphs (*continued*)

- Write numbers on the markers along the bottom to show how many people answered the question.

- Mark your results on the graph.

- Shade in the bars.

Title: _____

Number of Answers

- Write what you can learn about your topic by looking at the graph.

_____

_____

_____

_____

Name_____ Date_____

Compiling Notes into Outlines

To make an outline, you must begin with notes that you have taken on a certain topic. Look over your notes and decide what ideas you want to use as the main ideas. These will be the main headings in your outline. Under each main heading, you can list important details or information that explains or tells more about the main ideas.

- Think about an event in your life that was important to you. Write notes about what happened and your reaction to the event.

_____

_____

_____

_____

_____

_____

_____

_____

- Now, look over your notes and decide on one or two main ideas. Then decide what details go with each main idea. Fill in the outline below.

Topic: _____

Main heading: I. _____

Details: A. _____

                _____

                B. _____

                _____

                C. _____

                _____

Main heading: II. _____

Details: A. _____

                _____

                B. _____

                _____

                C. _____

                _____

Unit Wrap-Up

- How did you like this unit?

  ☐ I really enjoyed it.   ☐ I liked it.

  ☐ I liked some of it.   ☐ I did not like it.

- Was the unit easy or hard?

  ☐ easy   ☐ medium   ☐ hard

- Did you learn much during the unit?

  ☐ I learned a lot about courage.

  ☐ I learned a few new things about courage.

  ☐ I did not learn very much at all.

- Explain your last answer.

  _____

  _____

  _____

- What was the most interesting thing you learned about courage?

  _____

  _____

- What did you learn about courage that you didn't know before?

_____

_____

_____

- What did you learn about yourself as a learner?

_____

_____

_____

- What did you have to work on to become a better learner?

_____

_____

_____

- Which resources, such as books, magazines, interviews, and the Internet, did you use on your own as you investigated courage? Which was the most useful? Why?

_____

_____

Knowledge About Our Country and Its People

- This is what I know about our country and its people before reading the unit.

_____

_____

_____

_____

- These are some things I would like to know about our country and its people.

_____

_____

_____

_____

Reminder: I should read this page again when I get to the end of the unit to see how much I've learned about our country and its people.

UNIT 6 Our Country and Its People

Recording Concept Information

As I read each story, this is what I found out about our country and its people.

- "The First Americans" by Jane Werner Watson

_____

_____

_____

_____

_____

- "New Hope" by Henri Sorensen

_____

_____

_____

_____

_____

_____

- "A Place Called Freedom" by Scott Sanders

_____

_____

_____

_____

_____

_____

- "The Story of the Statue of Liberty"
  by Betsy Maestro

_____

_____

_____

_____

_____

_____

- "The Butterfly Seeds" by Mary Watson

_____

_____

_____

_____

_____

_____

- "A Piece of Home" by Sonia Levitin

_____

_____

_____

_____

_____

_____

- "Jalapeño Bagels" by Natasha Wing

_____

_____

_____

_____

_____

_____

_____

Our Country and Its People

Choose one of the areas of the country that "The First Americans" told about. Find out more about the Native American groups who lived there originally. Then fill in the information below.

- Area of the country: _____

- Name some of the Native American groups who lived there.

_____

_____

_____

_____

- Things I learned that were not stated in "The First Americans":

_____

_____

_____

_____

- Questions I have after learning more about these Native American groups:

_____

_____

_____

_____

_____

- Things I could do to find the answers to my questions:

_____

_____

_____

_____

_____

Our Country and Its People

Write the questions about our country and
its people that interest you on the lines.

_____

_____

_____

_____

_____

_____

_____

_____

_____

Which one of the questions interests you
the most?

_____

_____

Name_____ Date_____

Choosing Sources

It is important to know where to find the information you will need for your investigation. Use this page to write the best sources for finding information you need. Explain your reasons for choosing the source.

Investigation question: _____

_____

A good source of information is _____

_____

I would use this source because _____

_____

I can find this source _____

_____

Another good source of information is _____

_____

I would use this source because _____

_____

I can find this source _____

_____

UNIT 6 Our Country and Its People

A Place Near a River and Forest

In "The First Americans" you learned about how different Native Americans lived. You learned about their food, clothing, and homes, the ways they traveled, and what they did for fun. You learned how their lives were different depending on the kind of land in which they lived and the natural resources that they had.

Now think about how the location near the river and the forest helped Lars Jensen's family and the people who came to live in New Hope. Think about how people live and what they need to live, such as food, a home, and ways to travel. How could a river and the forest help people? Look back through the story "New Hope" to help you answer the questions.

1. What kinds of resources might a river provide?

   _____

   _____

   _____

   _____

2. What kinds of resources might the forest provide?

_____

_____

_____

3. What business did Lars Jensen start because of the river? How did this business bring more people to New Hope and lead to other businesses being built?

_____

_____

_____

_____

_____

_____

4. Why did lumbermen and farmers come to settle in the area where Lars Jensen did?

_____

_____

_____

_____

_____

5. What business did Lars Jensen start because of the lumbermen and farmers who came?

_____

_____

6. In the story of our country, barges and steamboats traveled down rivers carrying people and goods, such as lumber, over long distances. When the roads and railroads were being built, how might being near a river have made people decide to build a road or railroad near the town of New Hope? How might this have helped New Hope grow?

_____

_____

_____

_____

_____

_____

_____

7. What new questions or ideas do you now have about our country and its people? Write them here or put them on the Concept/Question Board. How do your new questions or ideas change or add to the first questions you had after reading "The First Americans"?

_____

_____

_____

_____

_____

_____

_____

UNIT 6 Our Country and Its People

Investigation Planning

Use the calendar to help plan your unit investigation. Fill in the dates. Make sure that you mark any days you know you will not be able to work on the investigation. Then choose the date on which you will start and the date on

Sunday	Monday	Tuesday	Wednesday

which you hope to finish. You may also find it helpful to mark the dates by which you hope to complete different parts of the investigation. Record what you accomplish each day.

Thursday	Friday	Saturday

Name_____ Date_____

Our Idea (or Conjecture)

Our investigation question:

_____

_____

_____

Conjecture (my first idea or explanation):

_____

_____

_____

_____

_____

  As you collect information, your questions
and conjectures might change. Return to this
page to record new questions or conjectures.

Using an Encyclopedia

One of the most helpful resources you can use when doing an investigation is an encyclopedia. An **encyclopedia** is a set of books with information on many topics, arranged in alphabetical order. Each book in the set is called a **volume**.

Here is an illustration of an encyclopedia. It has 20 volumes. Count the volumes.

- Use the illustration above to answer the questions below. Information about a person is arranged by the first letter of the person's last name. Write the volume letter or letters where you might find information about the following subjects.

1. Information about Denmark _____

2. Information about the history

   of blacksmithing _____

3. An entry on Laura Ingalls Wilder _____

Using an Encyclopedia (continued)

4. Information about New York _____

5. An entry on Henri Sorensen _____

6. Information about ferries _____

7. Information about horses _____

- Below are questions that can be answered by looking in an encyclopedia. For each question, write one or more entries, or subjects, under which you would look to find the information. For example, to answer the question, "What is the difference between a dog and a wolf?" you might look under "dog," "wolf," or "animals."

1. What kind of animal is a kangaroo? _____

_____

2. What is the difference between a parrot and

   a parakeet? _____

_____

3. Which city has more people living in it, New York

   or Los Angeles? _____

_____

4. Who invented baseball? _____

_____

The Starman Family and the Jensen Family: Alike and Different

Think about the story of the Starman family and the story of the Jensen family. Answer the questions below. You can look back over the stories to help you.

1. Think about where the Starman family came from, how they traveled, and what land or bodies of water they had to cross. Did they travel alone? Describe the Starman family's journey in the space below.

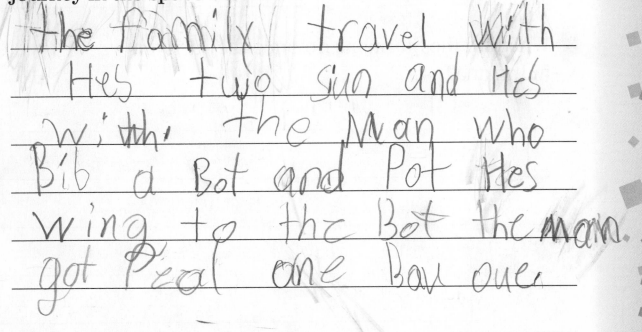

the family travel with
Hes two sun and Hes
with the Man who
Bib a Bot and Pot Hes
wing to the Bot theman
got Peol one Bou oue

2. Think about where the Jensen family came from, how they traveled, and what land or bodies of water they had to cross. Did they travel alone? Describe the Jensen family's journey in the space below.

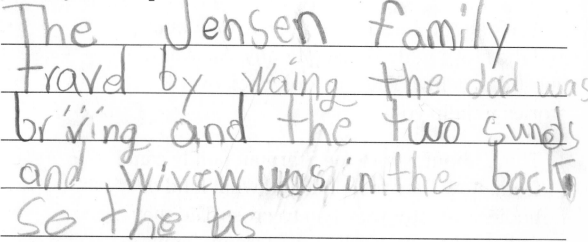

The Jensen family
travd by waing the dad was
briying and the two sunds
and wivew was in the back,
so the tas

3. What did the Starmans do once they arrived in Indiana?

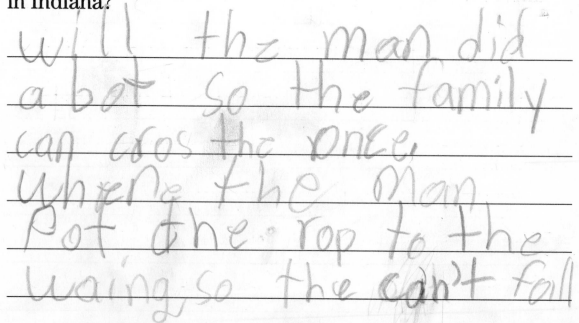

will the man did
a bot so the family
can cros the once,
when the man
got the rop to the
waing so the can't fall

4. What did the Jensen family do once they
arrived at the place by the river?

Wene the family got thay
thay where pepl taka Fire
uin thay got thay tary
wre Hrsed and pelpl
and House and Anmlin.
and threese and faler
and wotll.

5. Tell how the story of the Starman family and
the story of the Jensen family are alike and
different.

The Star Man family
Jenses family traveld
Star man family traveld
by bat and thay ars
traveled by ewaing

6. Do you think there were other families whose stories were like the stories of the Starmans and the Jensens? Explain your answer.

_____

_____

_____

_____

_____

_____

7. What ideas about our country and its people do the stories of the Starmans and the Jensens give you?

_____

_____

_____

_____

_____

_____

Interview a Citizen of Freedom

What other questions would you like to ask a
settler of Freedom? Write them in the space
below.

_____

_____

_____

_____

_____

Which of the questions you wrote could be
made better to give you better answers? Write
your reworded questions here.

_____

_____

_____

_____

_____

Needs and Plans

My group's question:

_____

_____

Knowledge Needs—Information I need to find
or figure out to help investigate the question:

A. _____

_____

B. _____

_____

C. _____

_____

D. _____

_____

E. _____

_____

Source	Useful?	How?
Encyclopedias		
Nonfiction Books		
Magazines		
Newspapers		
Videotapes, films, etc.		
Television		
Interviews, observations		
Museums		
Other		

UNIT 6 Our Country and Its People

Use Multiple Sources

Write your investigation question and your conjecture.

_____

_____

_____

_____

_____

There are many different sources you can turn to for your investigation.Complete the questions below about two possible sources you could use.

First Source: _____

- What type of information does this source contain?

_____

- What might you learn from this source about your question?

_____

_____

_____

- Find the name of one source of this kind (in a library) that you might be able to use in your investigation.

_____

_____

Second Source: _____

_____

- What type of information does this source contain?

_____

_____

- What might you learn from this source?

_____

_____

- Find the name of one source of this kind (in a library) that you might be able to use in your investigation.

_____

_____

Fiction vs. Fact

In the story "The Butterfly Seeds," you read about how Jake and his family moved to America. After crossing the ocean on a large ship, they docked in New York and had to go to Ellis Island. As they waited in a long line, they felt afraid because they weren't sure what was going to happen to them. They were checked to make sure they were healthy.

How is this story of Jake and his family like the true stories of real immigrants who came to America? One way to find out is to read what some of these real people wrote and to look at their real pictures. Write your answers to the questions below.

Give two examples of primary sources.

_____

_____

_____

Give two examples of secondary sources.

_____

_____

_____

Complete the chart to see how true Jake's story is compared to the real stories of the immigrants who came to America at that time long ago.

Write what happened to Jake and his family and tell how Jake felt when he arrived in New York. You can look back through the story to help you.
What happened to real immigrants and how did they feel when they arrived in New York? You can look back over the primary sources to help you answer the question.
How is what happened to Jake alike or different from what happened to the real immigrants?

UNIT 6 Our Country and Its People

A Special Trip

Moving from one place to another, or from one country to another, can make us feel excited or sad or even frightened. How would you feel if you were on a trip to begin a new life somewhere else? If you have ever moved, think about how you felt. Then think of the trips you have read about in this unit. Imagine yourself on one of these trips. Then write a letter to someone you left behind, telling about your feelings and experiences. Share the letter with a classmate or classmates.

Dear _____

_____

_____

_____

_____

_____

_____

_____

_____

Compile Notes into Reports or Summaries

At the end of "The Butterfly Seeds," the boy had many butterflies by his window box. Let's find out more about butterflies.

- Take notes for each heading below. Remember when you take notes to keep them short and use your own words most of the time. If you like the way something is written, write it word for word and put quotation marks around it.

The Life Cycle of a Butterfly

_____

_____

_____

_____

What Butterflies Eat

_____

_____

_____

_____

Butterflies Found in My Area

_____

_____

_____

_____

- Now use the notes you took to write a short report or summary about butterflies. Each heading should be a paragraph. Use extra paper if you need to.

_____

_____

_____

_____

_____

_____

_____

_____

_____

Name_____ Date_____

Taking Along a Piece of Home

Tell about a time when you went someplace for the first time or had to do something for the first time. For example, you might tell about going to school for the first time. Write how you felt and tell whether you took along something special and why. If you didn't take something special along, tell what you might have taken and why.

_____

_____

_____

_____

_____

_____

_____

_____

_____

_____

_____

Journeys: Alike and Different

Complete the chart to tell what is alike and different about the plot, the setting, and the main characters from "A Piece of Home" and "The Butterfly Seeds."

Plot:	How are events in the two stories alike and different?
Setting:	How is the setting in each story alike and different?
Character:	How are what Gregor and Jake do and feel alike and different?

Using New Technology

After you have conducted your investigation, you could use a form of technology—such as a computer, a video camera, or a color printer—to present your information.

Complete the questions below about using a form of new technology to help present information.

- **First Idea for a Presentation**

What would be one way to present your information without using new technology?

_____

_____

_____

_____

How could you use a form of new technology to help you present the same information?

_____

_____

_____

_____

- ## Second Idea for a Presentation

What would be another way to present your information without using new technology?

_____

_____

_____

_____

How could you use a form of new technology to help you present the same information?

_____

_____

_____

_____

Name _____ Date _____

Unit Wrap-Up

- How did you like this unit?

  ☐ I really enjoyed it.   ☐ I liked it.

  ☐ I liked some of it.   ☐ I didn't like it.

- Was the unit easy or hard?

  ☐ easy   ☐ medium   ☐ hard

- Did you learn much during the unit?

  ☐ I learned a lot about our country and its people.

  ☐ I learned a few new things about our country and its people.

  ☐ I didn't learn very much at all.

- Explain your last answer.

  _____

  _____

  _____

- What was the most interesting thing that you learned about our country and its people?

  _____

  _____

- What did you learn about our country and its people that you didn't know before?

  _____

  _____

  _____

- What did you learn about yourself as a learner?

  _____

  _____

  _____

- What did you have to work on to become a better learner?

  _____

  _____

  _____

- Which resources, such as books, magazines, interviews, and the Internet, did you use on your own as you investigated our country and its people? Which was the most useful? Why?

  _____

  _____

  _____